S0-ACL-766

Better By The Letter

Educator Edition

Sandi Washburn, M.A.

Enjoy !
SandiWash

This is a compilation of years of practice and implementation of ideas, studies both in and out of formal school settings, and serves as a guide only. Suggestions in this book are just that, suggestions. Please use caution, good judgement, and recognize the limits of the practices and/or yourself. Enjoy!

© 2020 Sandi Washburn

ISBN: 978-1-09831-082-0

All rights reserved.

Cover photo credit: Ahni Washburn

Dedication

This book is dedicated to my colleagues – a group of incredible and talented people that have inspired me to grow and learn, to fail and try again, to develop as a person as well as a student, and to share in the passion of teaching our youth.

Acknowledgements and Gratitude

To my amazing children, Hanna, Ahni, and Chloe, you 3 have given me such support and encouragement along the way; thoughtful critiques, formatting, and editing advice; and daily opportunities to practice and model the practices in this book. I am beyond blessed to be your mom. To my sister Laurie, always encouraging me to stretch and step out of my comfort zone, I thank you for the accountability checks and cheerleading you give in every conversation we have. Steve Bentley, thank you for your push and showing me a way to complete this project. And to Lucy Poe, thank you for the editorial support and perspectives you gave through the process. I truly appreciate the space you created for me to take the first step in sharing this book.

Introduction

First and foremost, thank you for picking up this book! It has been a work of love and I hope you find it a useful guide to practicing and finding some peace in your Every Day. I have been a student of the stress response, its purpose, its effects, its applications, and its manageability for over 20 years. I have practiced techniques in many settings – from student to teacher; from young adult to parent; from athlete to coach, and I continue to learn and practice. And I still don't have all the answers! But I do have some suggestions and strategies that I have found useful in my day-to-day life. In the following pages you will not see specific references to journals or books, but more general references to the phases, effects, and practices I have gathered from so many places in my life that I honestly can't pin it all down.

My greatest hope for this book is that it becomes a tool for you. A coffee-stained, dog-eared resource from which you learn a little, find a practical strategy, and use it. When that is the case, that means you have read, thought, and practiced; referred to, recalled, and reminded yourself that the greatest practice you can do for all the students you support, is to **take care of yourself**.

The term "self-care" often calls forth visions of massages, bubble baths, long walks on a beach (and if we're being honest here, we add a glass or two of wine into the equation). "Self-indulgent", "selfish", and "weakness" are words often used to describe it. The idea that self-care takes too long, that one only gets that on vacation, or that one needs to "earn" it also surfaces when I ask people to define or describe what self-care means to them.

But here's the deal – without regular down time, or intentional recovery time from a stressful event, the body and mind actually change. Those changes tend to be less than helpful.

You can't predict or prevent every stressor out there. But what you *can* do is learn to recognize how stress feels, how to use stress to your benefit, and how to manage your response.

The Stress Response

Stress happens. Just the word "stress" creates a response in some of us. Stimuli come at us every day from so many sources that we often don't even realize we are reacting. But stress itself isn't all bad. When we experience stress in small doses, it triggers effective levels of hormones to prompt us to move, to study, to compete, and to learn. When the stress levels get too high, we kick into a survival response.

At the *baseline* stage, you are relaxed and steady. At this point, you are just chillin' and going along with life in a calm and productive manner. You can easily access the thinking part of your brain (often referred to as the "new brain" or "rational brain"). This part of your brain, the pre-frontal cortex, is responsible for executive functioning. This is the ability or organize, to think ahead, to plan, to use professional judgement among other skills.

When you are *triggered,* you likely begin to feel changes start to happen. Hormones are released that signal the body to prepare for fight or flight. At this stage, you lose some of the ability to access the frontal cortex and begin to rely more on the survival response. You may notice you get antsy, nauseous, or easily distracted. At this stage, you might start firing off snarky responses to requests or comments. You may also find yourself focused, energized, and eager to tackle tasks or assignments.

As you hit _escalation_, the cascade of hormones signaling your body systems to move into survival mode continue to flood your body. You may notice you make louder and more aggressive responses to comments (maybe even including threats), muscle tension increases in your jaw, clenching of your fists, adopting a threatening posture, or running away. You may feel panic or be unable to finish or organize your thoughts. Access to your rational brain is at about 50% as your limbic brain is taking over and focuses on your survival.

When you hit the _peak stage_, all self-control goes out the window while comments fly, punches or items are thrown, or doors are slammed as you leave the situation. While here, you are unable to think rationally, to plan, or to be understanding and empathetic. Your limbic brain is in full control here. All of your energy is focused on your survival, and you are unable to consider consequences of your actions.

As you escape the stressful situation and the threat is gone, you _disembark_ and get off that emotional roller coaster ride. Your physical resources are exhausted, and your rational brain begins to come back on-line. You may find yourself highly emotional, crying or sobbing, or even sleeping as your body begins to clear out the excess hormones. Here the body begins to repair itself: blood pressure, heart rate, and breathing normalizes, hormone levels also normalize, and return to pre-stress levels.

In the _recovery_ stage, you may notice that you are able to reflect on the situation, consider what happened, problem solve, and feel remorse or a desire to repair any damage (to relationships or physical property) that may have resulted from the situation.

This natural and automatic response is a beautiful thing. It drives our survival. This response is designed to be a short-lived, quick acting response to danger. Think in terms of minutes. Physically we can't withstand the long-term flood of chemicals and changes in the body for extended periods of time (hours to days or longer). If we remain in a chronic stress state we experience symptoms like fatigue, fuzzy thinking, muscle aches, stomach aches, headaches, dehydration, over-or -under eating, sleep disturbances, and the like. Burnout, adrenal fatigue, depression, and anxiety may also crop up. You are at higher risk to experience frequent illness due to compromised immune systems, malnutrition symptoms due to compromised digestive systems, and many other maladies.

Practice:

Here is your first opportunity to practice: Take a few deep breaths, close your eyes, picture yourself in a situation that you categorize as stressful. It might be getting on an airplane or driving or riding in a car. It might be that first job interview. It might be watching your child fall in a sporting event. It might be an argument with a co-worker or family member. So many things bring on a stress response. So just pick one.

Are you picturing it? Set the scene including any other people, the weather, the sounds. Great.

Now, try to recall how you were feeling **physically**. Did you feel your muscles tighten, your jaw clench? Did you feel a pit in your stomach or did your face flush with color?

Open your eyes and bring your attention back to this book.

What did you notice?

Where are your thoughts going?

How did your body respond?

The reactions you felt are unique to you and your experience of stress. There is no right or wrong response. No two people respond the same! Understanding how you feel when under stress will help you figure out strategies that will help you mitigate the effects. Sometimes you need to slow the breath. Sometimes you need some gentle stretching of muscles or big body movements. Sometimes you may need to find something to focus on to be more present in the moment (and less lost in your worries of past or future events). As you get to know and understand how you respond to different stressful situations, you can create your own menu of strategies that work for you.

Become a Student of Self-Care

In the school setting where I have spent most of my professional career, teachers ask students to regulate their emotions, to plan and organize, to learn new things, to make friends. We put them in stressful states on purpose because that is when learning happens. We intentionally set students up for stress! Yet we rarely teach them how manage that stress.

The time has come to teach this.

Teaching starts with learning. We learn self-care and stress management by doing and then teach by example. This is not "just another thing" to add to your already full teaching plate. The beauty of teaching these skills is that you get the best results by modeling. That's right! You practice throughout your day. No lesson plans to create. No carving out extra time in your day for a formal lesson or creating small or whole group settings. Study your own triggers and reactions. Study different techniques to diffuse the effects of stress on your body. Learn what works for you and what skills you can use throughout your workday. Breathe. Stretch. Narrate what you are doing and move on.

Kids do what we do. When a student sees you using strategies in response to stressors, and that they help you stay emotionally regulated, that student will naturally begin to try out the skills or ask you about them, or even remind you to use one! Even if they don't adopt the skills, you will benefit by mitigating the effects of stress on yourself. Putting into practice your own self-management strategies during the school day will not only make you a happier more engaged teacher, but your students will also become happier more engaged students.

26 strategies to help you feel

Better By The Letter

Let's get started!

Awareness

Start with a breath. Just a breath. Inhale. Exhale

No changing it. No slowing it. No deepening it. Just breathe.

Pay attention to it. How does it feel? How does it sound? Where does the breath go?

When we pay attention to our breath, lots of things happen. One is that we focus on the here and now. We bring the focus to ourselves and thereby lose focus on external things: weather, other people, tasks, noises, frustrations, "what if's" and "should haves" and other worries.

When the focus is on the here and now, the present breath, you are unable to worry or ruminate over the past or future. When you are able to focus on the present with your breath, you give the signal to your brain that it can rest. The sentry on duty can take a break. You are safe.

Use this awareness exercise any time you find yourself getting wound up in the "what if" or the "should have" or other thoughts and worries. Take a breath. Remind yourself you are safe. You are right here. You are in control.

Breathe

Put one hand on your belly and one hand on your chest. Breathe evenly in and out. Deepen the breath each cycle, breathing in as long as you breathe out. Try to create an even rhythm to your breathing. You will notice that your breathing slows down as you focus on it.

The breath is a reflection of the nervous system: as the breath goes, so goes the nervous system. Think about when you exercise – your breath becomes shallow and rapid. When you are talking about or reading about, "hot button" issues (those that bring about passion, anger, or frustration), your breath becomes shallow and rapid again. When you are studying, preparing lessons, learning new skills, again your breathing becomes irregular, and you may find yourself holding your breath at times. These breathing patterns signal your brain to be on alert. This triggers the stress response.

There are times that we need a little stress, a little push to get things done. At a low level, the stress response gives us that: focus, drive, strength, heightened acuity of the senses.

Use the breath exercise to take control of your own nervous system and the response.

Alternate exercises: Play with these variations for 2-3 minutes at a time.

- Breathe in through one nostril, and out through the other
- Breathe in for a count of 4, and exhale for a count of 7
- Breathe in deeply through your nose, exhale with a loud sigh

C

Cross Your Midline

Reach your left hand over to tap your right shoulder or knee. Return the left hand to your side. Now reach your right hand over to tap your left shoulder or knee. Repeat this in an even rhythm for a count of 20 or for 30 seconds.

As you repeat the behavior, you are crossing the mid-line that runs up and down your body, splitting it in to right and left halves. Actively crossing this midline helps regulate the nervous system by coordinating the hemispheres of the brain to work together. Neurologically, you are "lighting up" areas of the brain associated with logic and rational thought. These areas are active in reading from left to right, so warming up this way before tackling that text book or new reading task may help!

Repeating rhythm and patterns in a calm and thoughtful way like this also calms the nervous system. Moving rhythmically and predictably like this signals the brain that you are safe.

Use this exercise when you are preparing for reading, writing, or any task that requires focus and linear thinking. You will be regulating the nervous system and allowing the rational thinking skills to be primed and available. You might even notice that you have automatically matched your movement with your breath.

Downward Dog

Get down on your hands and knees. While keeping both your hands on the ground, slowly (seriously, watch the dog. Go slowly. Take your time.) push back onto your feet, widening the space between your hands and feet, until you are in an inverted "V" position. Relax your neck, relax your shoulders, and breathe. Enjoy the upside down feeling, notice the change in blood flow, and how gravity feels in your body while in this position. Stand up (again, go slowly) when you feel ready.

Dogs have the right idea. Have you ever noticed how they stretch almost every time they get up? They go in to "puppy pose" or downward dog as they stretch out before going for a walk or investigating that dinner bowl.

This exercise hits many different stress points: the breathing naturally changes when gravity pulls differently on your body in space. Being upside-down moves the blood and lymph through your body (the lymph system depends on movement to function!). Being upside-down also changes your view of a situation, literally! This taps into a different area of the brain and allows creativity, openness, and awareness to expand. When paired with intentional breathing, you are regulating the nervous system while also allowing for more access to the rational part of the brain.

Use this exercise when feeling like you need a whole body movement, when you feel like you need a change in perspective, when you are looking for creative alternatives to a problem, or when feeling "stuck" or in a rut with your thinking.

Exhale.

Exhale completely.

Take a minute to breathe regularly. Notice how the inhale and exhale flow.

Next, take a regular inhale, but extend the exhale so that the exhale is longer than the inhale. Notice how much more breath you have left and can push out when you try.

Take 3 more breaths, extending the exhale each time.

When you lengthen your exhale, and really clear out the air in the bottom of the lungs, you again benefit in many ways. One has to do with the depth and stretch of the lungs themselves. This action activates receptors that don't often get called in to play unless you are regularly doing cardio training of some sort. Working the muscles around the lungs plays a role in overall health of those organs and vessels. Two, when the exhalation is forceful, as it is in the bottom of the exhale as you force out as much air as you can, the inhale becomes relaxed as the air comes in passively. The cycle naturally becomes deeper and slower, calming and regulating the nervous system response.

Use this exercise when you feel frustrated or stuck. Sometimes when in conversation or when teaching we run in to a wall where we feel misunderstood or unable to verbalize our thoughts clearly. Using a forceful exhale, which is followed by a passive inhale, can help calm the frustration and allow the clarity to return.

**Teens often naturally use this activity, paired with a loud vocalization – and sometimes an eyeroll! It is a natural response and works for the person using the strategy. I wouldn't recommend using it in class but understand that this similar behavior may be telling you that they are as frustrated as you in a given situation.

Flying Fun!

Reach your arms up above your head and stretch upward, as if reaching for the ceiling or sky, depending on where you are. Now let them float down, light as a feather, drifting slowly back to your sides. Reach up again, maybe adding a little lean from one side to the other with your hands up high. Now let them float back down again, until they get to your sides. Repeat this as often as you want to, but go at least 3 times.

We don't spend much time reaching up above our heads and getting our hands above our hearts, and this activity helps us change that up a bit. Changing that flow, taking a minute or two for playful imagination lights up different areas in our brains. Like some of the other exercises in this book, triggering other areas of the brain allows for creative solutions, for positive action, and for perspective taking

Use this exercise when feeling fatigued (mentally, emotionally, or physically), when unable to maintain focus of thought, or when you are in need of a creative boost for problem-solving. This may also benefit students before math exams, writing tasks, or social skills lessons.

Modifications to this exercise:

*pair breathing with the movements – breathing in as you reach up and breathing out as the arms float back down

*create a story to go with your movements -- you may be a bird soaring up to catch a thermal and then floating within it, a rocket blasting to space and floating in space or to a landing spot, a flower that is stretching toward the sun and then petals that reach out...whatever feels right to you at the time!

G

Gratitude.

Write down a list of things you are grateful for today. It doesn't have to be on fancy paper; or written in your best penmanship. Just jot it down on a sticky note, a napkin, a scrap paper...anywhere. There is magic not only in thinking about these things, but also in the act of writing.

Journal it. If you have a journal (or a spiral notebook or the like), grab it and start filling it in. By the end of the school year, I'll bet you have it filled up. And then you also have evidence that life really is good!

Text someone and tell them that you are grateful for something they did or shared with you. It might be some everyday thing we take for granted – having running water, having a bed to sleep in, having a choice of what to wear to work. It might be a compliment someone gave you, a flower you noticed on your way to school, or that a particular student "got it" in your math class.

Once you start your list, you'll find it easy to keep going! Spend just a few minutes a day jotting down thoughts of gratitude and see how your perspective changes.

It's a popular practice now; although, it's not a new one. Recent research demonstrates that practicing gratitude has positive effects on the brain. It affects the release of certain chemicals and creates a feeling of peace, of ease, and of harmony. If you have been under chronic stress and dwelling in the flood of chemicals released with that natural response, practicing gratitude has been shown to ignite healing pathways in the brain.

Use this exercise when you are feeling fatigued, worn down, or frustrated with the day. In class, you might start or end your day with a focus on gratitude. Students can write something on a scrap paper and put it in a jar. As they continue to add to it, they can pull one out and read it or use it for a writing prompt in class.

Haaaa Breath

Take a breath and exhale loudly, with attitude. As you exhale, vocalize a "Haaaa" and stretch it out to last as long as your breath. It's a bit like a loud sigh. Some of you may have practiced this in a yoga class or a breathwork course, as it is very beneficial and a great mood buster. This one is really fun if you have tweens around!

The active exhale with the noise is relaxing to the nervous system and can trigger a giggle or two as well (hence the mood-busting effect). The longer exhale signals the brain that things are under control and allows the "sentry" to take a break. This stops the stress chemical release and opens the door for the feel-good chemicals associated with giggling or laughing.

Try this exercise in between classes (most of you will be a little uneasy and want privacy the first few times) when your room is empty. Or even in the restroom. But once you practice this, and even invite your students to practice with you, you'll feel how much fun and effective this can be for all involved.

Imagine.

Sit in a quiet spot. Close your eyes and allow yourself to imagine. Create pictures in your mind of you being successful. It might be about teaching a difficult math concept. It might be a sports or athletic event. It might be trying something new like cooking a soufflé. Whatever it is, imagine it in detail – the sounds, the smells, the setting. Feel the movement in your body, how you are sitting, standing, running, breathing. Notice the temperature, the environmental noises around you in your imagined place. You may be alone or surrounded by others. Create as detailed a picture as you can.

Then notice the feelings – peace, pride, satisfaction, joy, elation. Breathe in those feelings. Flood your body with those positive emotions.

Imagery is a powerful practice and can be used to our advantage. Too often we imagine, or worry about, negative events or outcomes, and we are often validated in our worry. Our brains can't tell the difference between real or imagined events (have you ever woken up from a dream with your heart racing even though you were tucked safely in bed?). The body responds the same to actual experience as it does to imagined events. Intentional use of imagery, constructing and practicing successful events and repeating these patterns more often will result in positive outcomes.

Practice this before teaching a new concept, before an interview, or other performance related event. Take 3-5 minutes really constructing the scene, feeling all the positive emotions that go along with your success.

**Students will also benefit from trying this practice before tests, before presenting in front of the class, or other performance events.

J

Jellyfishin'

Yes, I said jellyfishin'. It's not really a word, but it sounds fun. Have you ever watched a jellyfish swim around in the ocean? Allow yourself to move as if you were a jellyfish or as if you were made of jello. Gracefully and slowly move like a jellyfish. Float your arms around, up, down, left, right. Wave, wiggle, wobble. Flow.

Begin to slow your breath to match your movements. Slow and easy. Fun and breezy.

Spend 2-3 minutes allowing this gentle ripple to flow from your arms to your hands and fingers as you stretch and contract them. Let it travel to your shoulders as you let them drop down. Even up to your head as you drop your chin to your chest.

Try this exercise after you have been sitting for a while, when you feel the stress building in your shoulders, or when you feel your attention span getting shorter. These are signs that you need to get a little movement going to feed your brain.

If you need a little pick-up, breathe a little quicker, and inhale longer than your exhale. If you are looking to slow down your body, slow the movements and the breath.

Knee lifts or knee bends

From a standing position, lift one knee up as high as you can. (Yes, one knee at a time. Alternate the legs, this isn't a jump). Lower that knee down and lift the other one. You can alternate fast or slow, depending on what your body needs at the time. Move faster if you need to get energized or wake yourself up a bit; slower and intentionally if you need to slow your racing thoughts or negative emotions.

This exercise brings movement to the lower half of the body, crossing the horizontal midline of your body. Activity like this brings a change in perspective and balance to the body and the mind.

If knee lifts aren't your thing, you can do knee bends (or squats) instead. You will get the same effect of perspective and balance as you are changing the horizontal plane as you squat down and return to standing. If you have knee issues, be cautious with this one, and be mindful of how deeply you bend.

Try this exercise when you are feeling "stuck" on a lesson plan, on a project, or in any situation that calls for a fresh perspective. If you need to walk away from a power struggle at work, head to the restroom stall or walk outside and give this exercise a whirl.

L

Laugh!

Laugh. Giggle. Belly laugh. Laugh out loud!

This might be a time to read a joke book, watch a short funny video, or listen to a comedy skit. Sharing a laugh with friends or family is extra beneficial as the energy from laughing often promotes even more laughter.

Laughter really is great medicine and is a free and readily available tool to help regulate our stress response. Once we tap into something funny and have a laugh, there is a release of chemicals that signal the nervous system to calm down from worry and to enjoy the moment. We snap out of the protective and negative mindset and are open to positivity and new perspectives. Perspective-taking is a frontal cortex skill, so being in this state indicates that our rational brain is back "on-line" and we are out of the fight or flight response.

**Nervous laughter is not the same. For some of us, a nervous laughter is an indicator of emotional stress and looks and sounds different than laughter from joy.

Try laughter when you have time to read, to talk, or listen, or share a story or time with someone that brings you joy. Forcing laughter can be difficult in a classroom situation and can create awkward moments (although these have often led to great laughing experiences as well!) Laughter is contagious though, so showing videos of babies or people laughing can often work to bring the laughs!

Movement

Move your body with intention. I'm not talking about the general movement we engage in during the day, like walking to the kitchen and back. I mean intentional movement. It might be a brisk walk around the school, the office, a track, or in a neighborhood. It might be doing some jumping jacks, or sit ups, or other calisthenics. It might be stretching, or dancing, or lifting.

Exercise is a powerful thought shifter, and an effective mood shifter. When you move your body, you stimulate your muscles and organs, your blood and lymph systems activate, and your breathing rate and depth changes. All this activity signals the release of chemicals that are related to happiness.

Intentional movement involves not only the physical movement, but also a focus on that movement and how your body responds. Pay attention to the way the limbs move, the inhale and exhale, the sensations in your whole body. Be present in the movement.

Try this when you are feeling tired or stuck. Movement stimulates more movement, and when we feel sluggish in our body, or blocked in our thinking, adding some movement is a quick and easy way to feel energized and clear-headed.

Note that the movement doesn't need to be extensive or intense. Simply being intentional and paying attention to the movement will do the trick.

N

Nosh

Yup, that's right. Nosh. Eat. Grab a snack. I'm *not* suggesting that you comfort eat, or stress eat! But, often under stress, eating becomes too infrequent or we make choices that actually create more stress! Fuel your brain with balanced and healthy options.

Eating can trigger not only our digestive systems, but also memories, habits, and neurochemical changes in the body. With this in mind, it is important to choose foods that will help reduce your stress in the short term without increasing the stress in the longer term. Preparing food with love, enjoying it without distraction, and giving yourself permission to take a break from the moment that is prompting the stress will be most beneficial. Paying attention to the smells, texture, taste, and sounds of eating for a few minutes provides not only nourishment to your brain, but also a sense of calm overall. This in turn signals your brain that you are in safe and in control allowing the "sentry" in our brain to stop with the cascade of fight or flight chemicals.

If you are a person that "forgets" to eat when stressed, set a reminder on your phone or have someone remind you to eat something every couple of hours. Prep snacks in small snack bags or reusable containers so that you don't have to wash, cut, or even choose what to eat.

If you tend to mindlessly eat a whole bag of cookies while you work, try a little food prep activity: package up a healthy option in snack size bags or reusable containers. Stop whatever you are working on or doing for the few minutes you eat the snack, really paying attention to what you are eating and how your body is feeling.

Orange magic!

Grab an orange (or any other citrus fruit that you can) and roll it around in your hands. Squeeze it a little bit to release some of the oils and the scent. Breathe deeply, smelling the fruit. Does that take you down memory lane? Remind you of simpler times, summer, or someone you enjoy being with?

Scents are tightly associated with memory and can send signals immediately to our brain that are calming or alerting. Orange oil is known for its uplifting and worry-reducing effects. It promotes cheerfulness and calm at the same time, so it is a great mood enhancer and a relaxant. As you squeeze the orange, or peel the fruit, you release the natural oils into your hands and the air, providing a natural source of peace-inducing aroma.

Try this during your morning or afternoon break at work. Roll the orange in your hands, peel it, and mindfully enjoy eating the fruit. You will tap in to the magic of the orange oil and provide a dose of natural carbohydrate and hydration to your body.

*Students also may benefit from having a citrus break before taking a test or learning a new academic concept.

Puzzle it!

Spend a few minutes working on a puzzle of some sort. Crosswords, jigsaws, word finds. Electronic or paper versions, it doesn't really matter. Just find something that taps your thinking in a different way.

Set a timer or pay attention to the time, breathe deeply, and give your brain a break from the work in front of you.

Try to schedule puzzle breaks in your day based on the activity. To wake up and get your thoughts focused, try the crossword or a number puzzle while enjoying your morning coffee. To take a break from technical reading or focused learning, try a word search. You might even find that you enjoy a good old-fashioned dot-to-dot that you can color in afterwards!

You will also benefit from a puzzle break if you find yourself in a tense situation with colleagues or family, debate or discussion that hits emotional buttons, or times that may even be a bit long and non-stimulating (long drives for sporting events).

Quick write.

Grab a pen and a piece of paper. It can be any writing utensil you feel like using; and any kind of paper you can find near you. Set a timer for 90 seconds and just write anything that comes to mind. No correction. No formal sentence structure or grammatical rules. Write out whatever is bogging you down, bringing you to the brink of the stress threshold, or fueling an inability to focus on the work you need to be doing. Get it out of your head and down on the paper. Release it from your brain.

When that timer goes off, put the pen down.

Breathe deeply and slowly 3 times.

On your last exhale, let those thoughts go.

There is some magic in physically putting pen to paper. It works the brain in different ways than typing on a computer or smart phone. It hits different areas in the brain than using a talk to text option. Once the thoughts are out of your head and down on that paper, you can put it away for a while and focus on the task at hand. Those words will be there, ready to be digested or processed (or burned or buried or whatever) when you have the time to attend to them. For now, just let them go and enjoy the peace.

Try this exercise when you find yourself unable to focus, when your mind is full of distractions, and put them out on the paper. This is also an effective tool to use when you are trying to come up with solutions or need a creative boost – put it all out on the paper and go back to what you wrote later.

Reach for the Stars

Reach high above your head with both arms. You can do this from a seated or standing position, whichever feels best for you. As you exhale, reach your left hand a little higher. On your next exhale reach the right hand up a little more. Continue this for 2 more breaths with each hand.

Next, reach your left hand out to your side as far as you can. Then reach out with your right hand as far as you can. Again, match this stretch with your breath – exhale and reach a little further with the left, and then with the right.

Reaching and stretching up is a movement that we don't often do in our day. We reach out, we reach down for things, but working above our heads just doesn't happen much. This overhead stretch not only stimulates our muscles and ligaments in ways we don't typically move, but also changes our position in space. As we move in different ways, we trigger different areas in the brain. When stressed, a general response is to "hunker down" and tighten our muscles in preparation for fight or flight. While this is helpful if we really do need to run or pounce, over the long run muscles tighten and shorten, resulting in less flexibility and fluidity in our movements. We get literally get ourselves physically rigid or stuck.

Use this overhead reach when you are feeling fatigued, stuck in your thinking, or defeated in your efforts. Reaching and expanding will bring a fresh look, a new perspective, and an energy to your work.

S

Snooze

Set a timer for 10 minutes or less. Lay down or stretch out in a recliner. Close your eyes.

You might count your full breath cycles, count during the inhale and exhale (lengthening the exhale), or listen to a guided meditation.

Closing your eyes, even trying earplugs or headphones, will allow you to shut out other distractions and give your brain a break from incoming stimuli. It gives your brain a break to restore and repair.

Sleep is so vital, so restorative, and so balancing to our brain functioning and stress management. In fact, that's another book. Until you read that one, practice good sleep hygiene: plan your sleep; create your schedule so you can get 7-9 hours regularly, meaning that you don't really "catch up" over the weekend.

Your brain and your body need consistent "off" time to recover and rebuild. Set your room up for sleeping with dark curtains, cozy bedding, "white noise" if you like, and air circulation. You will benefit in your overall stress management in a huge way once you practice getting regular sleep.

Now, close this book and get some sleep.

T

Tactile practice

Grab a pen, a coffee mug, a set of keys. Anything that is near you and can be held in your hands comfortably. With your eyes closed, focus on how it feels in your hands. The texture: is it smooth, bumpy, rough? Does it have ridges, layers you can discern by touch, edges that are sharp, round, smooth? Does it have moving parts? Is it cold, warm, hot? Is it heavy or light? Really take few minutes to focus on the object you are holding and see if you can learn something new about this everyday object.

By closing your eyes and focusing on an object in your hand, you are bringing your thoughts to a focus on the here and now. You will be unable to worry or fret about the past or future while you are doing this, which as you know by now is where we get most triggered into a stress response. Taking a minute to focus your mind on this object will give your brain another break from the constant guarding against danger, while also exercising your sense of touch and stimulating different area of your brain. Taking breaks like this increase creative thought and problem-solving skills.

Practice this exercise when transitioning from one activity to another – moving from studying to paying your bills, or from lesson planning to room design. Students may benefit from this type of activity within class when moving from whole group instruction to an independent task.

U

Up-sighting

From a sitting or lying position, take your gaze from the typical straight out in front of you, or even down at a screen or paper, and look up. Look at the ceiling, the sky, the tree above you. Find a position where you can rest your head against a backboard, back of a chair, wall, or the floor so you relax your neck.

Breathe. Notice.

Holding your head steady, roll your eyes up, to the left, to the right, and repeat. Continue to breathe slowly and notice what you see and feel.

This is another way of changing your perspective. Looking at things another way, literally. The action of moving your eyes while holding your head still also stimulates other areas of the brain and fosters creative thinking. The combination of resting your neck muscles, stretching your eye muscles, and slow deliberate breathing will ease you out of the stress mode, and open you up to clear thinking and effective problem solving.

Visit. Talk. Chat. Share conversation with someone.

Find someone you can just talk with. Go for a walk, meet for coffee, or even schedule to meet via computer or phone. Just connect with someone in a *verbal* conversation.

There is magic in using your voice box, your ears, and your eyes to convey ideas and interpret emotions. Exercising verbal conversation skills, whether it's small talk, or deep theorizing, benefits the body in many ways: it stimulates a variety of brain areas, affects breathing patterns, and impacts the release of emotionally regulated hormones. Now, "conversation skills" not only involves talking or venting or sharing your insights, but also (and most importantly) *listening* to the other person, considering alternate opinions and ideas, and attending to verbal and non-verbal language. It's a two-way street. By putting yourself in a situation where you share the back and forth volley of a conversation, where you can see-hear-feel the content, you connect. As social beings, this connection is vital to ward off potential anxiety, depression, and isolation.

Choose this strategy when you have been working alone for long periods of time; when you have been driving a far distance; if you have been binge-watching TV or been stuck in some social media; or just when you realize you haven't actually spoken with anyone for a while. Get up, get out, and visit. (Yes, even you introverts need to connect with people!)

W

Walk.

Walk anywhere. Walk backward. Walk slowly. Walk quickly. Just walk with purpose. Intentional movement brings your focus to the here and now, again kicking you out of the stress-filled behaviors of worrying or fretting about the past or the future. Just be right here; right now. And move.

The movement of walking helps your muscular, lymph, and nervous systems to regulate and work in harmony. As your nervous system calms, the muscles fire smoothly, and the lymph can move. Your lymph system depends on movement to clear out the toxins and dead cells it collects. So as you move with purpose, you benefit not only by clearing stuff out physically, but also emotionally as you focus on the steps you take, the direction you go, and the peace you breathe in as you go.

Get up and walk anytime you need a fresh perspective, a break from trying to solve problems, or if you are feeling sluggish. Try walking backward – it forces a different concentration for your mind and uses different muscles than typical for walking. Did you ever watch the "silly walks" on late night TV? There is something to that practice too! It again forces you to be present – planning, constructing, repeating patterns. And just a chance to be silly! Who doesn't love that?!

Make an X

Stand up. Stretch your arms up really high and wide like you are making a letter Y. Now move your feet apart, somewhere between shoulder-width and a sumo-style stance. Stretch all your limbs trying to make the biggest X you can. Add some movement to this by reaching out with your left hand to touch your right toes (or as close as you comfortably can). Stand back up. Stretch out wide to return to the big X. Repeat that move on the right side: right hand to your left toes. And back to the stretched out big X.

If you need little pick-me-up, you can repeat this sequence quickly. If you need a little slowing down of your thoughts or heart rate, repeat the sequence slowly.   Crossing both the vertical and the horizontal midlines brings clarity, focus, and a sense of calm to the brain. The rate you move through this action will bring up or slow the heart rate and stimulate the nervous system.

Use this exercise after sitting for long periods of time and you need to increase focus; between meetings when you need to switch thinking skills; or anytime you notice your thinking narrowing (unable to consider other options or solutions).

Yawn, yell, or yodel.

Yes. Three options here that all will do the same thing. Your choice depends on where you are and how appropriate they may be. Sometimes in the middle of teaching a class, it's just not cool to yell. Or when you are presenting brilliant information at a conference, a yawn just doesn't convey confidence. But, if you are teaching a class of middle schoolers and seem to be losing their attention, yodeling might do the trick!

These three vocalizations all work with the idea of changing the breathing pattern. Often when we are speaking, we tend to breathe in a short & quick pattern. When you can step out and yawn really big, or yell (with a long exhale), or even yodel, you send signals to your amygdala that things are safe and you are in control. This allows the brain to take a break from searching for trouble. Aside from athletic endeavors, most people are not aware of their breathing patterns and how they change based on everyday activities. Bringing that awareness in helps you learn to regulate your stress response throughout your day.

Z

Zip it!

This one takes practice. And a lot of it. Seriously.

Stop talking. Challenge yourself to practice really listening. It might be to listen to the sounds around you, to the lyrics in a song, to a person. Try setting a timer for 5 minutes and make no vocalizations during that time.

Staying quiet when others are talking is one of the most challenging behaviors for teachers (or almost any adult) to do when working with kids. I can almost guarantee you that if you try this practice, your stress levels will go down. When we really listen; to the world around us, to other people, or to music; and when we allow the space for the noise or words to sink in, magic happens.

When listening to a person without trying to give advice or a solution or an opinion, the speaker often solves their own question or concern – taking it off our plate and decreasing our stress. Or, when you wait to respond, you more often have a well thought-out and rational response (versus an emotional one) and are more helpful – easing the conversation and decreasing the emotional intensity and thereby our stress response. Frequently people want to be heard, not "fixed", so spending more time listening we mitigate the emotional intensity and meet the needs of those around us much more effectively.

Practice this strategy, well, as much as you can! Breathe, relax, and listen.

Table of Letters

A   Awareness – paying attention to the breath

B   Breathe – variations on belly breathing

C   Cross Your Midline – cross the perpendicular midline

D   Downward Dog – whole body stretch and movement

E   Exhale – lengthening the exhale of your breath

F   Flying Fun –exercise to reach and stretch above our heads

G   Gratitude – suggestions for practice

H   Haaa Breath – long and vocal exhalation exercise

I   Imagine – visualization practice

J   Jellyfishin' – playful movement

K   Knee lifts or knee bends – crossing the horizontal midline

L   Laugh – from a giggle to a guffaw, laughter is great medicine

M	Movement – intentional movement
N	Nosh – healthy options to feed your brain
O	Orange magic – uplifting scent and oils of citrus fruit
P	Puzzling – use the puzzles as a brain break
Q	Quick Write – a 90 second writing activity
R	Reach for the Stars – stretch and expand the body
S	Snooze – hints to create a sleep routine
T	Tactile Practice – focus on the tactile properties of an object
U	Upsighting – perspective change by looking up
V	Visit – the give and take of balanced conversation
W	Walk – intentional walking, playing with speed, steps, direction
X	Make an X – ways to cross midlines
Y	Yawn, yell, or yodel – options to change breathing patterns
Z	Zip it – practicing silence; leaving empty space in conversation